WORLD'S
STRANGEST

Produced for Lonely Planet by Plum5 Limited
Authors: Stuart Derrick & Charlotte Goddard
Editor: Plum5 Limited
Designer: Plum5 Limited
Publishing Director: Piers Pickard
Art Director: Andy Mansfield
Commissioning Editors: Catharine Robertson, Jen Feroze
Assistant Editor: Christina Webb
Print Production: Nigel Longuet, Lisa Ford
With thanks to: Jennifer Dixon

Published in August 2018 by Lonely Planet Global Ltd

CRN: 554153
ISBN: 978 1 78701 300 1

www.lonelyplanetkids.com
© Lonely Planet 2018

Printed in China
2 4 6 8 10 9 7 5 3 1

STAY IN TOUCH – lonelyplanet.com/contact
Lonely Planet Offices:
AUSTRALIA The Malt Store, Level 3, 551 Swanston St., Carlton,
Victoria 3053   T: 03 8379 8000
IRELAND Digital Depot, Roe Lane (off Thomas St.),
Digital Hub, Dublin 8, D08 TCV4
USA 124 Linden St., Oakland, CA 94607 T: 510 250 6400
UK 240 Blackfriars Rd., London SE1 8NW T: 020 3771 5100

WORLD'S STRANGEST

PLACES

Stuart Derrick &
Charlotte Goddard

PICTURE CREDITS

CONTENTS

INTRODUCTION

The world is full of beautiful and strange places for us to visit and marvel at. Some have been around for thousands of years, while others are more recent, but they all deserve a place on your bucket list.

This book ranks the strangest places on the planet to tell you all about...

⭐ The power of nature or the skills of the people who created them

⭐ How our world is constantly changing

⭐ The most mysterious locations in the world

Turn the page to start your journey to planet Earth's most strange and wonderful places, including...

⭐ The location so secret that we can barely tell you about it

⭐ The city where everything is underground

⭐ A post office that you'll need your swimsuit to visit

⭐ An underground cavern filled with giant crystals

⭐ A desert with mysterious messages that may be intended for aliens

... and many more!

STRANGEOMETER

The places in this book are all unique in their own ways, so we've used a special strangeometer to rank them. This is made up of four categories with a score out of 25 for each.

These categories are...

STRANGEOMETER

 UNIQUENESS — 17/25

 WOW FACTOR — 8/25

 MYSTERIOUSNESS — 12/25

 SURREAL FACTOR — 13/25

 STRANGEOMETER SCORE — 50/100

UNIQUENESS

Is there anything else like it in the world?

WOW FACTOR

Will it leave you and your friends open-mouthed in wonder?

MYSTERIOUSNESS

Do we really understand this place?

SURREAL FACTOR

Is it beyond belief, like something from a fantastic dream?

STRANGEOMETER SCORE

These are added up to get a strangeometer score out of 100!

#40

The question is, how did a group of pigs get to an uninhabited island? Nobody really knows. Some people think a group of sailors left them there, with plans to come back and eat them later. Or maybe they swam to the island from a nearby shipwreck.

Pig Beach's real name is Big Major Cay.

STRANGEOMETER

 UNIQUENESS — 14/25

 WOW FACTOR — 8/25

 MYSTERIOUSNESS — 9/25

 SURREAL FACTOR — 17/25

 STRANGEOMETER SCORE — 48/100

PIG BEACH

Around 15 adorable swimming pigs and piglets hang out on an uninhabited island in the Bahamas known as Pig Beach.

Bahamas

In 2017, local people were sad to see that several of the pigs had died. It's thought that they died from eating too much sand, after tourists threw tidbits on the beach for them. The local government wants to put stricter rules in place to stop people from feeding the pigs.

The dry heat and lack of rain in Arizona mean aircraft take a lot longer to rust and fall apart. Also, the hard desert floor is able to support the weight of the planes, so it doesn't have to be paved over.

Arizona, US

There are other plane graveyards in the US but this one is the biggest. It's 40 sq. mi. (10.5 sq km) in size.

STRANGEOMETER

 UNIQUENESS — 7/25

 WOW FACTOR — 19/25

 MYSTERIOUSNESS — 6/25

 SURREAL FACTOR — 17/25

 STRANGEOMETER SCORE — 49/100

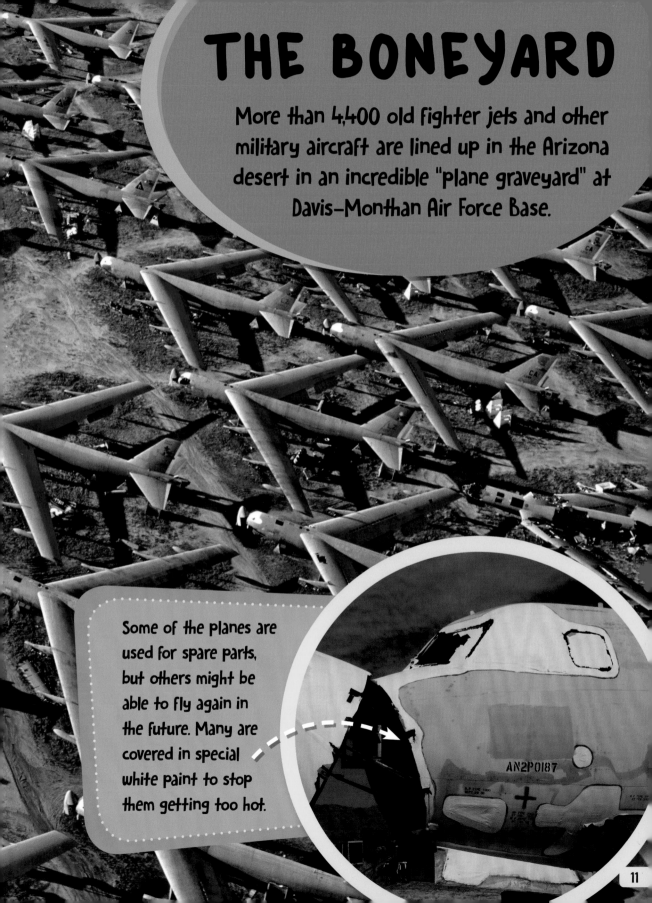

THE BONEYARD

More than 4,400 old fighter jets and other military aircraft are lined up in the Arizona desert in an incredible "plane graveyard" at Davis–Monthan Air Force Base.

Some of the planes are used for spare parts, but others might be able to fly again in the future. Many are covered in special white paint to stop them getting too hot.

AN2P0187

#38

In the past, people who lived on Tashirojima made silk, and they kept cats to chase mice away from precious silkworms. Now people think the cats are lucky, so they feed them.

People on Tashirojima like us so much there is a cat shrine in the center of the island. Dogs are banned from Tashirojima!

STRANGEOMETER

UNIQUENESS		7/25
WOW FACTOR		19/25
MYSTERIOUSNESS		6/25
SURREAL FACTOR		20/25
STRANGEOMETER SCORE		52/100

Japan

Tiny Aoshima, which is only 1 mi. (1.6 km) long, is also known as Cat Island. There are only around 15 people living there – but more than 120 cats!

CAT ISLANDS

There are a number of Cat Islands in Japan, where armies of furry felines rule the roost. In one of them, Tashirojima, visitors can even stay in cute huts built in the shape of cats!

New Zealand

Visitors can glide on a boat through the dark cave, where the only light comes from the galaxy of glowworms overhead. Although their twinkling lights are beautiful, the glowworms actually look like maggots!

#37

STRANGEOMETER

UNIQUENESS	9/25	
WOW FACTOR	19/25	
MYSTERIOUSNESS	8/25	
SURREAL FACTOR	19/25	
STRANGEOMETER SCORE	55/100	

Waitomo is made of two Maori words: *Wai* means "water," while *tomo* means "a hole in the ground."

Maori chief Tane Tinorau opened the caves to tourists in 1889, but the government took over the running of the caves in 1906. In 1989, they were returned to the descendants of the original owners, and many of them still work there as guides.

WAITOMO GLOWWORM CAVES

A starry wonderland of tiny living lights, New Zealand's glowworm caves were first explored in 1887 by a local Maori chief and an English surveyor.

#36

The lake is very salty. Some people think that the pink color comes from bacteria that live in the salt crusts.

Western Australia

STRANGEOMETER

 UNIQUENESS 9/25

 WOW FACTOR 19/25

 MYSTERIOUSNESS 10/25

 SURREAL FACTOR 21/25

 STRANGEOMETER SCORE 59/100

The water is safe to swim in, but nobody does, because the lake is so hard to reach. It can be viewed from above by helicopter, but aircraft are not allowed to land.

LAKE HILLIER

Scientists are not sure why this Australian lake is so peculiarly pink. The water looks more colorful from above but is still rosy when you put it in a glass.

Lake Hillier, which is pink, is not to be confused with Pink Lake, which is not pink! Pink Lake lies 78 mi. (125 km) to the east of Lake Hillier and lost its rosy color some time ago.

RAINBOW MOUNTAIN

This fantastic multicolored mountain, called Vinicunca, looks like someone has painted it, but the colors are completely natural.

Peru

Vinicunca is known as the "seven-colored mountain" by locals. Its amazing colors are made by thick stripes of mineral deposits across the mountain's sandstone rock.

Vinicunca is in the Cusco region of Peru. The colorful mountain was only revealed a few years ago when the ice that covered it melted. Visitors have to climb to a dizzying height of 17,000 ft. (5,200 m) to get this view.

Over time, the mineral deposits in the rock reacted with oxygen in the air to produce a rainbow of colors.

STRANGEOMETER

UNIQUENESS		12/25
WOW FACTOR		17/25
MYSTERIOUSNESS		10/25
SURREAL FACTOR		21/25
STRANGEOMETER SCORE		60/100

COOBER PEDY

The town of Coober Pedy is so incredibly hot that most people prefer to live in underground caves. There are underground art galleries, churches, museums, bars, and hotels, as well as houses.

Coober Pedy has a golf course, but it gets so hot during the day that most people play golf at night with glow-in-the-dark balls!

STRANGEOMETER

UNIQUENESS		16/25
WOW FACTOR		14/25
MYSTERIOUSNESS		11/25
SURREAL FACTOR		21/25
STRANGEOMETER SCORE		62/100

Coober Pedy is around 500 mi. (800 km) from the nearest city.

Australia

In 1915, a teenager discovered opals in Coober Pedy. Around 150 million years ago, the town was underwater, but when the water gradually moved away, minerals from the seabed turned into the multicolored gemstones. Most of the world's opals come from Coober Pedy.

CHOCOLATE HILLS

They may look like something out of Willy Wonka's chocolate factory, but don't try snacking on these hills – despite the name, they are made of mud, limestone, and grass!

The Chocolate Hills are found on the island province of Bohol in the Philippines. They appear on the island's flag, behind a picture of two arms dripping blood. The picture represents a friendship ceremony that took place between a Spanish explorer and a local leader hundreds of years ago.

The green grass on the hills turns brown like chocolate in the summer. There are more than a thousand mounds that range from 100-400 ft. (30-120 m) high.

STRANGEOMETER

 UNIQUENESS — 9/25

 WOW FACTOR — 17/25

 MYSTERIOUSNESS — 16/25

 SURREAL FACTOR — 21/25

 STRANGEOMETER SCORE — 63/100

Philippines

Locals say the mounds were formed by a giant water buffalo that stole villagers' crops. In revenge, they left out spoiled food for the beast to eat, which made it sick, and the hills were formed when it pooped many times! Another story says the hills were formed from the dried tears of a sad giant.

#32

PAMUKKALE

It looks like a frozen waterfall, but it's actually a hot-water spring! Pamukkale, the name of these striking white terraced pools, means "cotton castle" in Turkish.

Turkey

there are 17 hot springs at Pamukkale. In the past, they were used for cleaning wool. At the top of the steps is a pool that Cleopatra is said to have swum in. You can swim in it, too – just wade carefully around the Roman ruins that have fallen in!

The water at Pamukkale has been pouring down the mountain for millions of years, collecting in pools on the way. It's filled with chalky white minerals, which it leaves behind, making the pools look like marble steps. the shimmering steps are actually made from a rock called travertine.

STRANGEOMETER

UNIQUENESS		7/25
WOW FACTOR		24/25
MYSTERIOUSNESS		9/25
SURREAL FACTOR		24/25
STRANGEOMETER SCORE		64/100

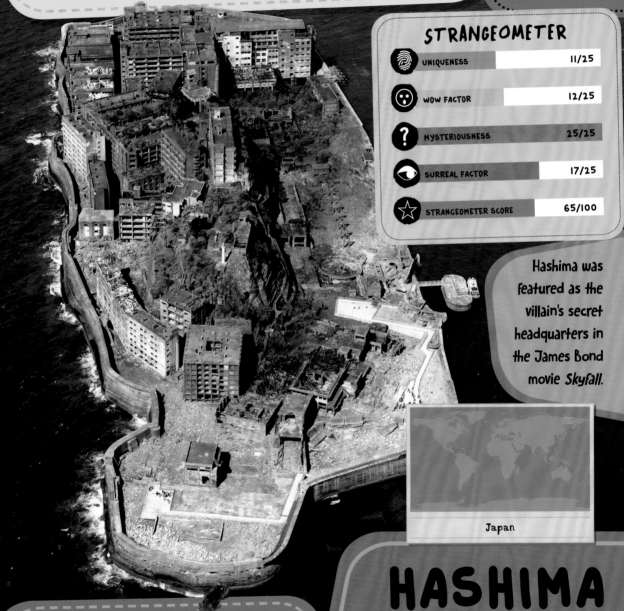

Once upon a time, Hashima was packed with 5,300 coal miners and their families, living squeezed together in apartment blocks on an island the size of 13 soccer fields. When the mines closed, the island was abandoned. Empty apartments still have posters on their walls and contain dusty and broken TVs and telephones.

STRANGEOMETER

UNIQUENESS		11/25
WOW FACTOR		12/25
MYSTERIOUSNESS		25/25
SURREAL FACTOR		17/25
STRANGEOMETER SCORE		65/100

Hashima was featured as the villain's secret headquarters in the James Bond movie *Skyfall*.

Japan

HASHIMA

Hashima's concrete buildings include apartments, a school, hospital, movie theater, and swimming pool. But nobody has lived there since 1974.

Hashima is known as Battleship Island because of its shape. Nobody was allowed on the island from 1974 to 2009, but now people can visit a small part of it. The rest is too dangerous – the buildings might collapse on your head!

QUIZ

See if you can answer these questions on the ten places you've just learned about!

Where in the world is this?

4.

1. Where is Pig Beach?

2. How many planes are in Arizona's plane graveyard?

3. Why did the people of Tashirojima originally keep cats?

6.

What do locals call Vinicunca?

Where do most of the world's opals come from?

7.

8.

5.

Why do people think Lake Hillier is pink?

Where in the world is this?

10.

9.

What did people do at the springs of Pamukkale in the past?

When did people last live on Hashima Island?

The local radio station broadcasts crab bulletins to keep listeners up-to-date on the crabs' whereabouts.

CHRISTMAS
ISLAND

Every year, the beaches and roads of Christmas Island turn into a crimson carpet when more than 50 million red crabs migrate from their rainforest homes down to the sea to lay their eggs.

It takes around a month for the larvae to develop. Then, millions of cute baby crabs clamber ashore. They take about nine days to make the long march inland.

The crabby critters cause chaos on their way to and from the beach, stopping traffic, puncturing tires, and wandering into people's houses. Islanders have built a 16 ft. (5 m) high crab bridge to help crabs cross a busy road, as well as 31 crab underpasses.

STRANGEOMETER

 UNIQUENESS — 24/25

 WOW FACTOR — 23/25

 MYSTERIOUSNESS — 3/25

 SURREAL FACTOR — 16/25

 STRANGEOMETER SCORE — 66/100

Indian Ocean

AREA 51

US military base Area 51 is in the middle of the dusty Nevada desert, far away from any town. The perfect place to hide weird and top-secret activities!

STRANGEOMETER

 UNIQUENESS — 17/25

 WOW FACTOR — 10/25

 MYSTERIOUSNESS — 25/25

 SURREAL FACTOR — 15/25

 STRANGEOMETER SCORE — 67/100

The US government has always been very secretive about Area 51 and did not admit it even existed until 2005. Airplanes are not allowed to fly over it. Scientists there work on top-secret projects.

NELLIS BOMBING AND GUNNERY RANGE
RESTRICTED AREA

NO TRESPASSING
BEYOND THIS
POINT

PHOTOGRAPHY IS
PROHIBITED

WARNING

Restricted Area

It is unlawful to enter this area without
permission of the Installation Commander.
Sec. 21, Internal Security Act of 1950, 50 U.S.C. 797

While on this installation all personnel and
the property under their control are subject
to search.

Use of deadly force authorized.

The US Air Force bought
the Area 51 site in 1955.
The base is built on the
site of disused lead
and silver mines.

Nevada, US

There are all kinds of stories
about Area 51. Some people think it is
used to store alien spaceships that crashed into Earth.
Others say it's the site of secret meetings between aliens
and the government. It's also been said that scientists there
are inventing time travel and teleportation devices.

#28

Poland

STRANGEOMETER

 UNIQUENESS **12/25**

 WOW FACTOR **16/25**

 MYSTERIOUSNESS **20/25**

 SURREAL FACTOR **20/25**

 STRANGEOMETER SCORE **68/100**

There are around 400 pine trees in the Crooked Forest, most of which have a weird curve in the trunk, making them look like a hook. Strangely, the Crooked Forest is part of a larger forest where the rest of the trees are growing perfectly normally.

CROOKED FOREST

This spooky woodland is full of creepy, curved trees. Nobody knows what makes them grow in such a strange way.

There are lots of ideas about why the trees are curved. Some say it was because of heavy snow, while others say the young trees were flattened by tanks in World War II. Another idea is that the trees were made to grow that way by farmers who wanted to use them to make curved planks for ships.

Almost all of the curves on the trees point the same way – north.

#27

UNDERWATER POST OFFICE

If you want to mail a letter in the world's only underwater post office, make sure it's waterproof! To reach it, you have to dive 10 ft. (3 m) under the sea.

Vanuatu

> WE USE A SPECIAL STAMP THAT MAKES A MARK UNDERWATER WITHOUT INK.

The Post Office is just off the coast of Hideaway Island, one of the 83 islands that make up the Republic of Vanuatu. A flag floating in the water above the Post Office shows when it's open. Even when it's closed you can mail a postcard in the mailbox attached to the Post Office.

STRANGEOMETER

UNIQUENESS	22/25
WOW FACTOR	20/25
MYSTERIOUSNESS	7/25
SURREAL FACTOR	20/25
STRANGEOMETER SCORE	69/100

Visitors to Vanuatu can also mail a letter in a mailbox on the fiery rim of a volcano. Imagine mailing a letter with molten lava exploding in the air just a few feet away!

Venezuela

STRANGEOMETER

UNIQUENESS		17/25
WOW FACTOR		23/25
MYSTERIOUSNESS		15/25
SURREAL FACTOR		15/25
STRANGEOMETER SCORE		70/100

#26

Lake Maracaibo has more lightning strikes than anywhere else on the planet. Storms occur 260 nights a year, each one lasting for around nine hours.

There was no lightning between January and March 2010 and people thought it might have stopped altogether – but the spectacular electric storms were soon back again.

The lightning lake is so famous it's shown on the flag of the state of Zulia, home to Lake Maracaibo, and is mentioned in the state anthem!

LAKE
MARACAIBO

They say lightning never strikes the same place twice, but that's certainly not true at Lake Maracaibo. Here, every square mile receives around 180 lightning strikes every year!

The Hidden Beach is also known as Playa del Amor, which means the "beach of love."

People say the hole that created the beach was made when the Mexican government carried out secret bomb tests. Nobody lives on the Marieta Islands, but you can take a boat across to enjoy the crystal waters and white sands of this secluded cove.

HIDDEN
BEACH

The Hidden Beach is invisible from the outside. The only way to reach it is to swim through an 80 ft. (25 m) tunnel connecting it to the Pacific Ocean.

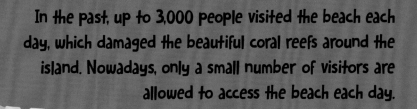

In the past, up to 3,000 people visited the beach each day, which damaged the beautiful coral reefs around the island. Nowadays, only a small number of visitors are allowed to access the beach each day.

STRANGEOMETER

 UNIQUENESS — 20/25

 WOW FACTOR — 21/25

 MYSTERIOUSNESS — 10/25

 SURREAL FACTOR — 20/25

 STRANGEOMETER SCORE — 71/100

Marieta Islands, Mexico

#24

MENDENHALL ICE CAVES

You can only reach these magical ice caves by clambering over a 13 mi. (21 km) glacier, located some 12 mi. (19 km) from Alaska's capital, Juneau.

The view is always changing as melting water running under and through the ice creates new caves, and existing caves collapse as the glacier melts.

Rising temperatures mean the glacier is melting – it is almost 2 mi. (3.2 km) smaller than it was in 1958. Visiting the stunning caves can be very dangerous, as there is always a chance that the icy blue ceiling could collapse on top of you.

STRANGEOMETER

UNIQUENESS		18/25
WOW FACTOR		24/25
MYSTERIOUSNESS		10/25
SURREAL FACTOR		20/25
STRANGEOMETER SCORE		72/100

Alaska, US

MUDHDHOO ISLAND

Maldives

Mudhdhoo Island is home to a truly amazing glow-in-the-dark beach. The shining specks are made by tiny shellfish the size of sesame seeds.

The beach doesn't always look like this - it's only when the sparkly little critters come out to play. Similar displays can be seen in other places around the world, such as the Caribbean.

During World War II, Japanese soldiers collected the sci-fi shellfish from the ocean and used the light to read maps and other papers at night. The light was bright enough to see by but not so bright that it would show enemy soldiers their location.

STRANGEOMETER

UNIQUENESS		18/25
WOW FACTOR		24/25
MYSTERIOUSNESS		12/25
SURREAL FACTOR		19/25
STRANGEOMETER SCORE		73/100

#22

Kamchatka, Russia

Part of the valley wall is known as Stained Glass, because it is tinted with reds, yellows, greens, and blues by a mix of soils and plants.

STRANGEOMETER

 UNIQUENESS — 20/25

 WOW FACTOR — 20/25

 MYSTERIOUSNESS — 15/25

 SURREAL FACTOR — 19/25

 STRANGEOMETER SCORE — 74/100

VALLEY OF THE GEYSERS

The Valley of the Geysers boasts more than 40 geysers spouting hot water into the air, as well as many boiling springs, hot lakes, and mud volcanoes.

Further upriver from the Valley of the Geysers lies Death Valley. It is filled with poisonous gases that kill off birds, plants, and animals.

In 2007, a huge landslide buried much of the valley and destroyed many of the geysers. The landslide also created some new geysers, as well as a new, turquoise lake.

#21

New Zealand

A traditional way to cook food in the area is to place fresh ingredients in baskets woven from flax and lower them into the boiling pools. There's no need for an oven!

TE PUIA

Te Puia is home to the largest geyser in the southern hemisphere. It erupts once or twice every hour, shooting boiling hot water up to 98 ft. (30 m) in the air.

Te Puia is famous for its boiling pools of mud. One pool, Ngā mōkai-ā-Koko, is between 20-33 ft. (6-10 m) deep. The steaming mud reaches temperatures of up to 203°F (95°C).

STRANGEOMETER

 UNIQUENESS — 21/25

 WOW FACTOR — 21/25

 MYSTERIOUSNESS — 12/25

 SURREAL FACTOR — 21/25

 STRANGEOMETER SCORE — 75/100

QUIZ

See if you can answer these questions on the ten places you've just learned about!

3. In what direction do most of the tree trunks in the Crooked Forest point?

How deep is the Underwater Post Office?

1. Where in the world is this?

4. When did the US government admit that the top-secret military base Area 51 existed?

2.

Where in the world is this?

6.

Why are the Mendenhall Ice Caves dangerous?

8.

7.

5.

On how many nights a year does Lake Maracaibo have lightning strikes?

What makes the beach on Mudhdhoo Island glow?

9.

10.

What colors make up the Stained Glass part of the Valley of the Geysers?

How often does Te Puia's largest geyser erupt?

The catacombs were created more than 230 years ago, when Paris ran out of space to bury the dead. Bones were moved into the ancient and sprawling stone mines underneath the city.

OSSEMENS DE L'EG
ET DU CLOÎTRE D
CAPUCINS S. HONOR
LE 29 MARS 180

CATACOMBS

The creepy catacombs 66 ft. (20 m) below the streets of Paris are filled with the bones of around 6 million people tightly packed on top of one another.

The tunnels were used by members of the French Resistance during World War II to hide from the Germans. The Germans also used the tunnels as a bunker, to shelter from attack.

The bones of Charles Perrault, who wrote *Little Red Riding Hood*, *Cinderella*, and *Sleeping Beauty*, are thought to be somewhere in the catacombs.

STRANGEOMETER

 UNIQUENESS — 23/25

WOW FACTOR — 20/25

 MYSTERIOUSNESS — 13/25

 SURREAL FACTOR — 20/25

 STRANGEOMETER SCORE — 76/100

#19

The salt covering the ground was left behind when a prehistoric lake evaporated thousands of years ago. There are 11 billion tons of salt at Salar de Uyuni, forming amazing patterns on the ground.

When it rains, a thin layer of water covers the salt flats and they are turned into a giant mirror.

Bolivia

SALAR DE UYUNI

The dazzling salt flats of Uyuni stretch for 4,000 sq. mi. (10,582 sq km). They are very high up – 11,700 ft. (3,565 m) above sea level.

STRANGEOMETER

UNIQUENESS		22/25
WOW FACTOR		23/25
MYSTERIOUSNESS		9/25
SURREAL FACTOR		23/25
STRANGEOMETER SCORE		77/100

At Salar de Uyuni you can stay in a hotel made entirely of salt. The walls are made of salt, the tables are made of salt, and even the beds are made of salt!

#18

LIVING ROOT BRIDGES

Villagers in India came up with a clever way to cross fast-flowing rivers and streams in the rainy season – living root bridges.

One of the most famous root bridges is the Umshiang Double-Decker, which is actually two bridges on top of each other. It is 180 years old.

Meghalaya, India

Villagers encourage rubber tree roots on opposite sides of streams to join and form a bridge. You have to be patient when you are making a root bridge – they take 15 to 20 years to grow.

STRANGEOMETER

UNIQUENESS	19/25
WOW FACTOR	22/25
MYSTERIOUSNESS	15/25
SURREAL FACTOR	22/25
STRANGEOMETER SCORE	78/100

EYE OF THE SAHARA

The Eye of the Sahara is a huge bull's-eye feature in the middle of the desert. It is 25 mi. (40 km) wide, but it was only noticed when astronauts were taking pictures of the Earth from space.

At first, scientists thought the Eye of the Sahara was a crater formed after an asteroid had smashed into the Earth. Now they think it might be the result of a volcanic eruption.

Mauritania

STRANGEOMETER

UNIQUENESS		21/25
WOW FACTOR		22/25
MYSTERIOUSNESS		14/25
SURREAL FACTOR		22/25
STRANGEOMETER SCORE		79/100

The Eye of the Sahara has become a landmark for astronauts. Even though you can't really see the formation from the ground, people still visit this remote area. You can even stay in a hotel in the middle of the eye.

#16

There are around 4,000 lancehead vipers on Snake Island. Locals say the dangerous snakes were put on the island by pirates to guard their treasure, but they actually evolved there over thousands of years.

STRANGEOMETER

 UNIQUENESS   20/25

 WOW FACTOR   23/25

 MYSTERIOUSNESS   12/25

 SURREAL FACTOR   25/25

 STRANGEOMETER SCORE   80/100

Brazil

Snake Island was cut off from the mainland around 11,000 years ago. the snakes that lived there did not have to fear any predators – but they also didn't have any prey to hunt on the ground. So they learned to slither up trees and eat birds.

SNAKE ISLAND

Brazil's Ilha da Queimada Grande, also known as Snake Island, is breathtakingly beautiful, but no one is allowed to visit because it is infested with one of the most poisonous snakes in the world – the golden lancehead viper.

The land is being ripped apart by the movement of huge plates under the surface of the Earth.

Afar, Ethiopia

STRANGEOMETER

 UNIQUENESS — 21/25

 WOW FACTOR — 23/25

 MYSTERIOUSNESS — 14/25

 SURREAL FACTOR — 23/25

 STRANGEOMETER SCORE — 81/100

The Erta Ale volcano, known as the "gateway to hell," has one of only six lava lakes in the world.

The desert is covered with salt plains up to 2,600 ft. (800 m) thick. It's impossible for most plants and animals to survive there, but local people with camel caravans have crossed the burning landscape to mine huge blocks of salt for centuries.

DANAKIL DESERT

With violent volcanoes, scorching temperatures, and lakes of yellow sulphur, Africa's Danakil Desert is one of the most spectacular places on Earth.

#14

GIANT'S CAUSEWAY

The Giant's Causeway is made of tall stone columns that look like they have been hammered into place. They fit together so closely it's hard to slide a knife between them.

Northern Ireland, UK

According to legend, the Irish giant Finn MacCool was challenged to a fight by the Scottish giant Benandonner. Finn built the causeway across the sea so the two could meet. But Benandonner got scared and ran away, tearing up the path behind him.

The causeway was actually formed when a flow of lava from an ancient volcano cooled as it hit the sea, around 50 million years ago.

STRANGEOMETER

UNIQUENESS	21/25
WOW FACTOR	24/25
MYSTERIOUSNESS	14/25
SURREAL FACTOR	23/25
STRANGEOMETER SCORE	82/100

Most of the 40,000 columns that make up the causeway are around 20 ft. (6 m) high, although some soar to 82 ft. (25 m). Most are hexagonal, but some have four, five, seven, or eight sides.

The rock is around 360 ft. (110 m) long. The different colors in the wave are made from spring water running down the rock and dissolving minerals.

STRANGEOMETER

	UNIQUENESS	21/25
	WOW FACTOR	24/25
?	MYSTERIOUSNESS	15/25
	SURREAL FACTOR	23/25
★	STRANGEOMETER SCORE	83/100

Local tribes believed Wave Rock was created by the Rainbow Serpent, an Aborigine god.

WAVE ROCK

It looks like a tall ocean wave about to break over your head, but Wave Rock is really a 50 ft. (15 m) granite cliff.

Australia

Scientists think ancient tribes dragged some of the massive stones that make up Stonehenge for 140 mi. (225 km), all the way from Wales. They might have rolled them along on logs or stone balls. Those must have been some very important rocks!

England, UK

STONEHENGE

The ancient circle of giant stone slabs in the middle of Salisbury Plain has puzzled people for centuries. Parts of Stonehenge are around 5,000 years old.

The Stonehenge we see today is smaller than it used to be. Some of the stones have been removed over the years.

STRANGEOMETER

 UNIQUENESS 21/25

 WOW FACTOR 21/25

 MYSTERIOUSNESS 25/25

 SURREAL FACTOR 17/25

 STRANGEOMETER SCORE 84/100

Nobody knows what Stonehenge was for. Some people think it was a temple. Others say it was a kind of prehistoric computer for predicting eclipses. There are lots of other ideas as well!

#11

STRANGEOMETER

 UNIQUENESS — 22/25

 WOW FACTOR — 23/25

 MYSTERIOUSNESS — 18/25

 SURREAL FACTOR — 22/25

 STRANGEOMETER SCORE — 85/100

Namibia

The Ugab Gate into Skeleton Coast National Park is adorned with two huge skulls and crossbones.

Sailors call this 981 mi. (1,579 km) stretch of coastline the Skeleton Coast because local winds and ocean currents have pushed ships and the carcasses of animals toward the shore.

SKELETON COAST

Namibia's ghostly Skeleton Coast is lined with the bones of long-dead whales and the crumbling wrecks of ships that met their doom on the sandy shore.

One ship, the *Eduard Bohlen*, seems to be wrecked in the middle of the desert. It's about 1,600 ft. (500 m) from the ocean! That's because the ship was wrecked more than 100 years ago, and since then, the ocean has retreated, and the desert has expanded.

QUIZ

See if you can answer these questions on the ten places you've just learned about!

3. How long does a living root bridge take to grow?

Who first discovered the Eye of the Sahara?

1. How many people's bones are in the Paris catacombs?

4.

2. Where in the world is this?

6. What kind of lakes should you look out for in Africa's Danakil Desert?

7. 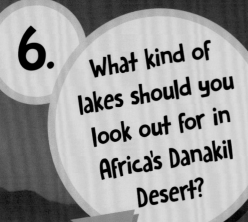 Where in the world is this?

5. What poisonous snake inhabits Snake Island?

8. Why is Wave Rock striped?

9. How old is Stonehenge?

10. How did the Skeleton Coast get its name?

#10

One of the ships that disappeared in the triangle was the USS *Cyclops*, which vanished without a trace in 1918. Five torpedo bombers disappeared inside the triangle in 1945, and a search and rescue seaplane sent to look for them also disappeared.

Bermuda Triangle, North Atlantic

Some people think that the vanished ships and aircraft were taken by aliens, and some say magic is involved. Others, such as the US Coast Guard and ship insurer Lloyd's of London, say there are no weird reasons for ships and planes going missing in the area. What do you think?

STRANGEOMETER

UNIQUENESS 21/25

WOW FACTOR 15/25

MYSTERIOUSNESS 25/25

SURREAL FACTOR 25/25

STRANGEOMETER SCORE 86/100

BERMUDA TRIANGLE

The Bermuda Triangle is a spooky area of ocean in the North Atlantic. Aircraft and ships are said to disappear there under mysterious circumstances.

#9

STRANGEOMETER

 UNIQUENESS — 23/25

 WOW FACTOR — 25/25

 MYSTERIOUSNESS — 16/25

 SURREAL FACTOR — 23/25

STRANGEOMETER SCORE — 87/100

WHITE DESERT

Visiting Egypt's fantastic White Desert will make you feel as if you have stepped onto the moon. The color of the sand ranges from snow-white to cream.

When the moon is full, the white desert gives off an eerie glow.

It's hard to believe, but this desert was once the bottom of a sea. Fossilized sea creatures are embedded in the sandstone.

Centuries of sandstorms have carved the chalk rock into alien-looking statues. Some of the "statues" have been given names – among them the mushroom, the chicken, and the ice-cream cone.

Al Farafrah, Egypt

#8

STRANGEOMETER

 UNIQUENESS — 25/25

 WOW FACTOR — 23/25

 MYSTERIOUSNESS — 20/25

 SURREAL FACTOR — 20/25

 STRANGEOMETER SCORE — 88/100

Visiting Pompeii is like going back in time – everything is frozen at the moment it was buried on August 24, AD 79. People can wander the cobbled streets, visiting houses, shops, temples, public baths, and an amphitheater.

Pompeii was a bustling city, with at least 150 bars, 25 public water fountains, and a swimming pool. The ancient Romans left graffiti all over the walls of Pompeii. Some of it is very rude!

POMPEII

Nearly 2,000 years ago, the city of Pompeii was buried under more than 20 ft. (6 m) of ash after nearby Mount Vesuvius erupted.

Most of the people who lived in Pompeii escaped into the countryside when the volcano erupted.

Italy

#7

SPOTTED LAKE

Every summer, this amazing lake gets seriously spotty. The hot sun evaporates some of the water, revealing around 400 colorful polka-dot pools.

British Columbia, Canada

The different colors are caused by different minerals, including magnesium, silver, and titanium, which get left behind when the water evaporates. The mud between the pools smells like rotten eggs!

STRANGEOMETER

UNIQUENESS	25/25
WOW FACTOR	24/25
MYSTERIOUSNESS	17/25
SURREAL FACTOR	23/25
STRANGEOMETER SCORE	89/100

The lake is sacred to First Nations people in Canada and the United States. Visitors are asked not to trespass on tribal land.

The tunnel is 4,000 ft. (1,200 m) long, about 16 ft. (5 m) high, and 13 ft. (4 m) wide. If you were driving through it, you wouldn't want to meet a car coming the other way! The views through the windows that are cut out of the rock are spectacular, and the tunnel is now a popular tourist attraction.

STRANGEOMETER

UNIQUENESS		24/25
WOW FACTOR		24/25
MYSTERIOUSNESS		19/25
SURREAL FACTOR		23/25
STRANGEOMETER SCORE		90/100

Before the tunnel was built, the only way to the village was an exhausting journey up 720 mountain steps.

China

GUOLIANG TUNNEL

This incredible tunnel was carved into China's Taihang Mountain by villagers in 1977. It links the village of Guoliang with the outside world.

#5

DARVAZA
GAS CRATER

Locals call this sinister pit of boiling mud and flames the Door to Hell. It has been burning for more than 40 years.

The crater is the size of a soccer field and reaches temperatures of 1,832°F (1,000°C).

Turkmenistan

STRANGEOMETER

UNIQUENESS		24/25
WOW FACTOR		23/25
MYSTERIOUSNESS		25/25
SURREAL FACTOR		19/25
STRANGEOMETER SCORE		91/100

It's thought that when scientists started drilling for oil here in 1971, they released huge amounts of methane gas by accident, which made it hard to breathe. They were worried about the gas exploding, so they set it on fire to get rid of it – but there was a lot more than they expected.

The Great Blue Hole was once a cave on dry land during an ice age, when sea levels were much lower than today. When glaciers melted and made the sea levels rise, the cave collapsed and was flooded.

The Great Blue Hole is very popular with divers due to its crystalline waters, abundance of sharks and coral, and stalactite-filled caves.

GREAT BLUE HOLE

This gigantic circle of deep blue, lying within a shallow sea of light colors, is a sinkhole that plunges 410 ft. (125 m) into the murky depths.

The water at the top of the hole is salty but at the bottom it's fresh. Divers see the water shimmer as they pass the area that divides the salty surface from the freshwater depths.

The Great Blue Hole is more than 1,000 ft. (300 m) wide!

STRANGEOMETER

UNIQUENESS		22/25
WOW FACTOR		25/25
MYSTERIOUSNESS		20/25
SURREAL FACTOR		25/25
STRANGEOMETER SCORE		92/100

Belize

#3

Scientists have found organisms trapped inside the crystals. They think the life forms are still alive, even though the tiny creatures have been sleeping for thousands of years.

STRANGEOMETER

 UNIQUENESS — 25/25

 WOW FACTOR — 25/25

 MYSTERIOUSNESS — 22/25

 SURREAL FACTOR — 21/25

 STRANGEOMETER SCORE — 93/100

CAVE OF THE CRYSTALS

This beautiful but deadly cave, 1,000 ft. (300 m) below the Earth's surface, contains some of the largest natural crystals ever found.

The biggest crystal is 40 ft. (12 m) long and weighs 60 tons.

Naica, Mexico

The spectacular crystals may look like ice, but in fact the cave is incredibly hot. To explore down there, scientists had to invent special suits that work like fridges.

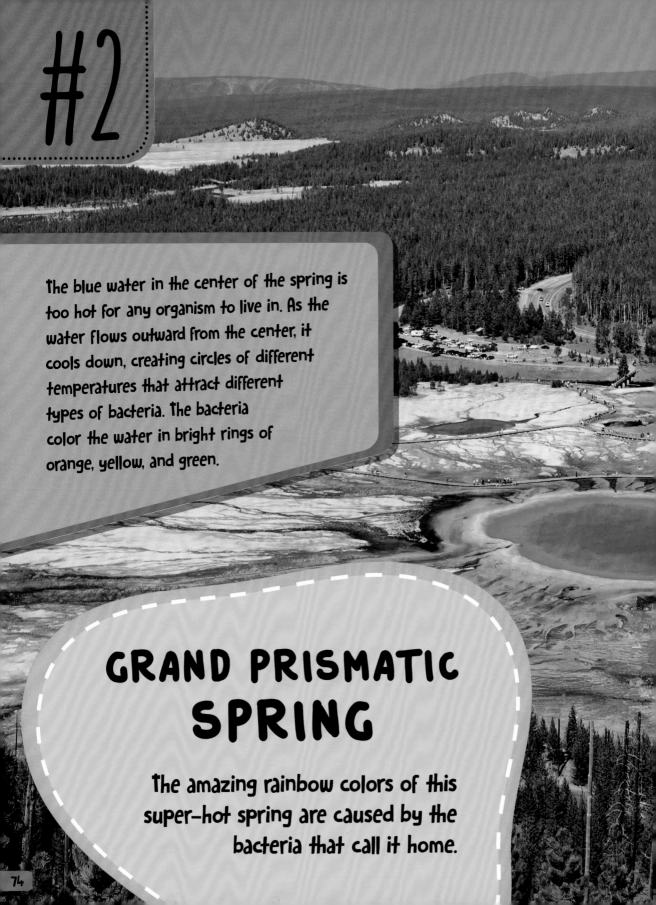

the blue water in the center of the spring is too hot for any organism to live in. As the water flows outward from the center, it cools down, creating circles of different temperatures that attract different types of bacteria. the bacteria color the water in bright rings of orange, yellow, and green.

GRAND PRISMATIC SPRING

The amazing rainbow colors of this super-hot spring are caused by the bacteria that call it home.

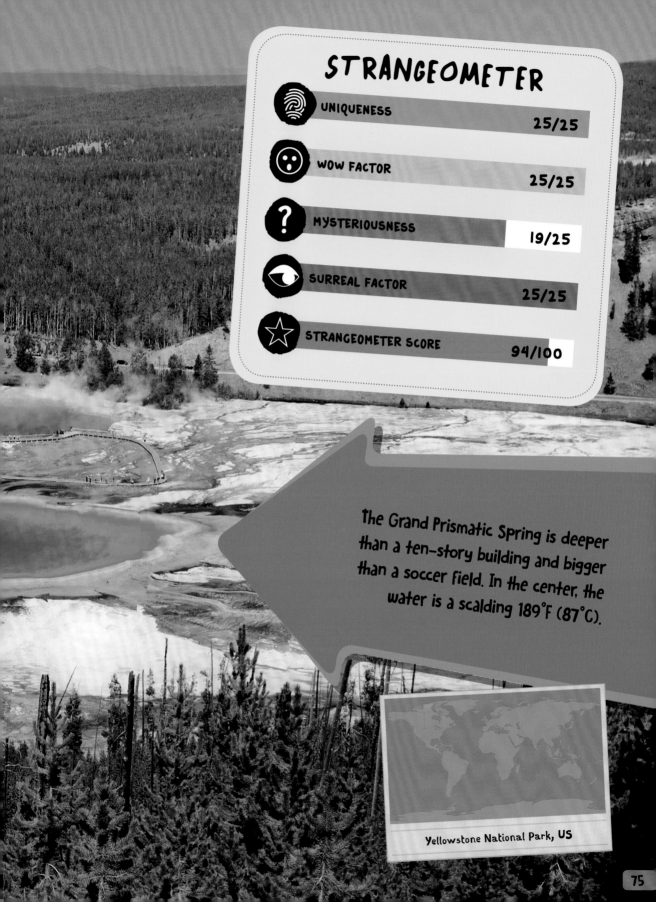

STRANGEOMETER

UNIQUENESS — 25/25

WOW FACTOR — 25/25

MYSTERIOUSNESS — 19/25

SURREAL FACTOR — 25/25

STRANGEOMETER SCORE — 94/100

The Grand Prismatic Spring is deeper than a ten-story building and bigger than a soccer field. In the center, the water is a scalding 189°F (87°C).

Yellowstone National Park, US

#1

The drawings were made more than 2,000 years ago, but people only started to notice them about 100 years ago, after airplanes were invented. That's why some people think the ancient Nazca could fly. Others say some of the lines were landing strips for alien spaceships!

Peru

The mysterious drawings cover a huge area of around 174 sq. mi. (280 sq km). There are about 300 different figures, including animals and plants. Some of the lines are 100 ft. (30 m) wide and stretch for more than 5.5 mi. (9 km).

NAZCA LINES

The incredible Nazca Desert in Peru looks like a page from a giant's sketchbook. But what made an ancient race draw pictures that can only be seen from the sky?

Some experts think the Nazca used the drawings to predict the position of the stars, while others say the symbols were a way of talking to their gods. But it's still a perplexing mystery!

STRANGEOMETER

UNIQUENESS		25/25
WOW FACTOR		25/25
MYSTERIOUSNESS		25/25
SURREAL FACTOR		25/25
STRANGEOMETER SCORE		100/100

QUIZ

See if you can answer these questions on the ten places you've just learned about!

1. What's unusual about the Bermuda Triangle?

2. Where in the world is this?

3. What volcano erupted, covering Pompeii in ash?

4. How many colorful pools make up Spotted Lake in Canada?

6. When did the Darvaza gas crater begin burning?

7. How wide is the Great Blue Hole?

8. Why do scientists have to wear special suits in the Cave of Crystals?

5. How did people get to Guoliang before a tunnel was built in 1977?

9. Where in the world is this?

10. How many different figures make up the Nazca Lines?

ANSWERS

1. SHIPS AND AIRCRAFT ARE SAID TO HAVE DISAPPEARED THERE.
2. EGYPT'S WHITE DESERT 3. MOUNT VESUVIUS 4. ABOUT 400
5. BY CLIMBING 720 MOUNTAIN STEPS 6. 1971 7. 1,000 FT. (300 M)
8. BECAUSE IT IS SO HOT 9. GRAND PRISMATIC SPRING 10. ABOUT 300

79

GLOSSARY

amphitheater	a round or oval open-air building with rows of seats surrounding a central area where shows are performed
bacteria	tiny organisms (living things) that are all around us
catacomb	an underground passage or tunnel used to bury the dead
coral	a marine animal that stays in one place under the sea and forms a hard, rock-like substance
eclipse	when one object in space moves between two others, blocking one from view – mostly used when the moon blocks our view of the sun
evaporate	to heat water up so that it turns into steam and rises into the air
fossilized	preserved in rock after millions of years
geyser	a hot spring that sometimes erupts, sending a huge column of water and steam into the air
glacier	thick ice that stays frozen year after year
graffiti	drawing or writing on a public wall or other surface, usually done illegally
hemisphere	one half of a ball, or sphere – used to describe the northern or southern halves of Earth
hexagonal	six-sided
lava	molten, or melted, rock that spills out from underground when a volcano erupts
mineral	naturally occurring substance that is not a plant or animal, obtained from the ground or under the ground
predator	an animal that hunts and eats other animals
prey	an animal that is hunted and eaten by other animals
shrine	a holy place of worship
silkworm	caterpillar that produces silk
stalactite	a formation that looks like an icicle hanging down from the roof of a cave, formed by water dripping and leaving a mineral deposit behind